KV-372-912

Floating the Woods

KEN COCKBURN

Luath Press Limited

EDINBURGH

www.luath.co.uk

First published 2018

ISBN: 978-1-912147-33-5

The author's right to be identified as author of this book
under the Copyright, Designs and Patents Act 1988 has been asserted.

The paper used in this book is recyclable. It is made
from low chlorine pulps produced in a low energy, low emission
manner from renewable forests.

Printed and bound by Bell & Bain Ltd., Glasgow.

Typeset in 11 point Sabon

© Ken Cockburn 2018

£4-00

KEN COCKBURN is a poet, translator, editor and writing tutor based in Edinburgh. After several years at the Scottish Poetry Library, since 2004 he has freelanced in schools, colleges and community settings, and has collaborated with visual artists on book, exhibition and public art projects. www.kencockburn.co.uk

By the same author:

Souvenirs and Homelands, Scottish Cultural Press 1998
The Order of Things, pocketbooks 2001 (edited, with Alec Finlay)
Intimate Expanses, Carcanet 2004 (edited, with Robyn Marsack)
Tweed Rivers, platform projects & Luath Press 2005 (edited, with James Carter)
Feathers & Lime, The Caseroom Press 2007 (translated)
On the flyleaf, Luath 2007
Centum, Fremi Books 2008 (with David Faithfull)
Overheard Overlooked, The Caseroom Press 2011
Ink, University of Abertay Press 2011 (with *~in the fields*)
Snapdragon, The Caseroom Press 2012 (translated)
The Road North, Shearsman 2014 (with Alec Finlay)
Veined with Shadow Branches, Sarah Myerscough Gallery 2014 (with Andrew Mackenzie)
Silence Before Speech, Knucker Press, 2016 (with Dina Campbell and Jane McKie)

For Alice and Isobel, of course

Contents

Acknowledgements

My thanks to all those who contributed to the conception, composition and publication of these poems: Stefan Baumberger, Nicole Heidkte, Luke Allan, Alec Finlay, Gair Dunlop, Lise Bratton, Graeme Murray, Claire Pençak, Mary Bourne, Peter McCarey, Susan Humble, Zoë Fothergill, Cat Outram, Tim Fitzpatrick, Maoilios Caimbeul, Saeko Yoshikawa, Stephen Henry Gill, Hisashi Miyazaki, Mike Collier, Janet Ross, Hazel Weeks and Sonia Ferras-Mana.

My thanks also to the following organisations which commissioned and/ or exhibited some of the poems: Royal Botanic Garden Edinburgh, Crailing Community Orchard, Northlight Arts, Artlink Edinburgh and Lothians, Scottish Poetry Library, Edinburgh Printmakers Workshop, Friends of Aden Country Park, National Trust for Scotland, the Wordsworth Trust and Kamikoro Bunko.

Some of these poems have appeared previously in print and online: in the periodical *Contemporary Literary Horizo*n; in the books *ink* (University of Abertay Press), *Backwater Republic: An imaginary community in the River Tay* (Gair Dunlop), *Scotia Extremis* (Luath), *Scotia Nova* (Luath), *Centum: 100 Years of Baillie Gifford 1908–2008* (Fremi Books), *Andrew Mackenzie: Veined with Shadow-Branches* (Sarah Myerscough Gallery), *there were our own there were the others* (morning star and Trust New Art/ National Trust); and on skying-blog.blogspot.co.uk, company-of-mountains.com, thesyllabary.com, cleikit.com, scotiaextremis.wordpress.com and castlegardenofwatertobeyond.wordpress.com. My thanks to all the editors involved.

I'd like to thank especially Alec Finlay and Angus Reid, who separately have encouraged, and cast usefully critical eyes over, these poems and this collection over an extended period. I am very grateful to Creative Scotland for an Artist's Bursary, which assisted some of its writing and editing.

Ken Cockburn
March 2018

Norm

So what's the norm in this neck of the woods?
Greetings and leave-takings for example,
pats, dabs, cheek-kisses, handshakes, embraces,
toasts, tips, quips, queues, curses, table manners,
neckwear, nightwear, refusals, condiments,
punctuality and superstitions,
the etiquette of stimulants, when not
to use the informal second person,
what's for breakfast, shop-talk, the latitude
or lack thereof accorded foreigners.

Forth

*We loved to watch the passing ships and make guesses
as to the ports they had come from.* – John Muir

a coracle of willow and skins beneath a changeable sky

a Roman flotilla edging north to Ultima Thule

a Viking longship breaking open the honeyed south

a Genoese galley blockading the castle

the Great Michael floating the woods of Fife

Sir Patrick Spens sailing the king's guid schip

the widowed queen's fleet arriving in thick mist

the brig Covenant of Dysart bound for the Carolinas

the clipper Isabella bringing tea into Leith

a herring-laden zulu tacking for Fisherrow

a U-boat periscope scanning the waves

the crude oil tanker Seadancer's flag of convenience

Orkney

we sail past Stroma's empty fields
the maidens grind the sea-gods' salt
binoculars to scan the scene
the latent power the races hold

divers down among the wrecks
I don't know what it is I've found
a haar drifts in across the rocks
the crab's blue shell fades in the sun

the Romans came and saw and left
Vikings named themselves in runes
a hoard of shards the dig unearthed
the sacred grove is made of stone

unfurl your banner to the breeze
starlings wheel across the sky
a spotted orchid in the verge
the wind is in the blades and flags

Credit
Alcinous to Odysseus

What can I say? My daughter comes across
you lurking naked – naked! – by the shore
and you have nothing to say for yourself
but some nonsense about nymphs and monsters.

You've made enemies of at least two gods
and yet now you ask me brazenly to
provide a ship and crew so you can reach
Ithaca, whence you came. Apparently.

Were I to take an interest in your scheme
I'd need to take a leap of faith, and that –
I operate in the real world, and this
smacks too much of fiction. Make-believe. Still...

An Alphabet of Blues

Arcadian-blue describes a sky in which clouds are gathering on the horizon.

Bauhaus-blue describes a sky heavily influenced by Modernism.

Camouflage-blue describes a sky trying its best to be inconspicuous.

Dysart-blue describes a sky which matches exactly the bluest of the sea-beams at the harbour.

Everyday-blue describes a sky taken for granted.

Fauve-blue describes a sky painted any colour other than blue.

Gloaming-blue describes a sky about to vanish.

Hume-blue describes a sky lacking all discernable trace of a divine beyond.

Ink-blue describes a sky articulated in the fields.

Jam-jar-blue describes a sky arranged above a wild-flower meadow.

Kirkcaldy-blue describes a sky above Stark's Park at the moment the home team scores.

Linoleum-blue describes a sky perceived as much by smell as by sight.

Miralles-blue describes a sky seen from the windows of Committee Room 5 in the Scottish parliament building.

Nettle-blue describes a sky just after it has begun to rain heavily.

Orange-blue describes a sky hallucinated through a necklace of windows.

Partan-blue describes a sky reflected in rock-pools.

Quagmire-blue describes a sky from which rain has been falling for days.

Ricochet-blue describes a sky through which a military plane is flying. Has flown.

Suprematist-blue describes a sky punctuated by Ian Hamilton Finlay in 1965.

Translator's blue describes a sky which is more at home elsewhere – smirr on Skiathos, azure above Arran.

Ume-blue describes a sky seen through the first plum-blossom of spring.

Vintner's blue describes a sky whose complexity demands a specialised vocabulary.

Watermark-blue describes a sky that is barely noticeable.

Ex-blue describes a sky which was there a moment ago.

Yester-blue describes a sky heavy with nostalgia.

Zed-blue describes a sky seen only in dreams.

Yen to See Different Places
A Romantic Haiku Machine

beneath these rocky heights
the lake's clear breast...
this fine old ruin

from gloomy raptures to
the arbour'd strand...
sepulchral yew

beneath the mountain's misty throne
the lonely down...
making improvements

from tall cliff and cavern lone to
boughs, and a low eminence...
a beached skiff

beneath precipitous peaks,
bank, bush and scaur...
the slender mountain-ash

from yon sequestered valley to
airy and romantic paths...
this rude and ruinous tower

from noble ravine to
silver, begirt with copsewood…
an air of majesty and dejection

        from savage grandeurs to
        where the horses drink their fill…
        memorial of a warlike age

from wild cascade to
the swollen stream…
a tinkle of bells

        from gloomy magnitude to
        shaggy heath…
        opening a vista

never scene so sad and fair…
where banks are placid…
sheltered by an ancient oak

        from steep and solitary rocks to
        groves deep and high…
        simplicity of rural habits

from inaccessible glen to
the willow'd shore...
under the greenwood tree

        from rugged dell to
        the stormy firth...
        scattered pine

down from the hills to
dark'ning heath...
the spectacle of May

Backwater Republic

The island breathes
in and out

slowly

like an old Chinese sage
lost in the hills.

*

As the tide ebbs

the city recedes.

*

Eider ducks eat
pebbles with mussels

to mill the shells
which means they shit

mosaics.

*

Each edit
the tide makes
is definitive

until the next one.

*

Everything on the shore
is a multiple

except for this
pine cone.

*

What's left of the folly
can serve as a windbreak.

*

Flow-tide
the island's edges

themselves become islands
settled by seabirds.

A Wee Word of Advice from the Empire

It's not difficult.

Listen. You worship
who you like BUT
the Emperor's a god
AND I want the taxes in
by the new moon.

Alright?
If it's not
it won't be just me
and Valerius here
come next time.

Seven Questions

What is seven?

seas and sleepers
sorrows and sisters

brides and brothers
magnificent samurai

pillars of wisdom
and ages of man

the days of creation's
labour and leisure

godly virtues
and deadly sins

the lost wonders
of the ancient world

of hills you need for a city
the requisite number

Who are the Romans?

the wolf-twins
and Trojan Aeneas

Etruscan kings
and republican consuls

razers of Carthage
and lovers of Egypt

translators of Greek
and crossers of Rubicons

emperors long-lived
or four to the year

bearers of laurels
and builders of frontiers

instigators and keepers
of *mare nostrum* and *pax Romana*

What is an emperor?

one acclaimed and not
whatever else a king

whose first act is
to deify his predecessor

who must not just maintain
but extend the empire

whose authority depends
on placating his army

who navigates between
virtue and debauch

whose thumb grants
reprieve or execution

to whom all poets, exiled or not
dedicate their works

What is a wall?

a unilateral declaration
of binary division

a line drawn in the sand
and fortified

a lasting reminder
that we're not all in this together

informal resentment
and official suspicion

a register
of comings and goings

a project to keep your own
onside and occupied

an immutable frontier
time can't help snigger at

What is a barbarian?

one who reckons wealth in cattle
and honour in raiding

prefers fighting his neighbour
to standing beside him

offers a tribute
only when pushed

remembers enough
not to write things down

has stone calendars
and bone implements

builds brochs and duns
in lochs and glens

makes the most
of forests and mosses

What are Edinburgh's seven hills?

a hinterland
of unreal estate

urban meadows
and untended suburbs

a thronged trig-point
and hillside sun trap

a library of barkbooks
composed by lovers

a cruising spot
and an unfenced drop

vantage points
and a field of monuments

a shallow burn
and a shady grove

What is Roman Edinburgh?

Hume's simple Roman tomb
in Calton Burial Ground

the unbound *fasces*
of the parliament

the Christians as those of the Roman church
on the pediment of St Patrick's

Finlay's baskets of olives and grapes
on the south-facing terrace of Hunter Square

Stoddart's betogaed Hume
burnished by superstition

the museum altars
to Mercury and Fortuna

the Cramond lioness
exhumed from the silt

Bob the Roman

We can't see Rome every day
and the thought of mis-spending so much time
among a most ridiculous set
of gamesters to no purpose –

I seek an unconstrained and noble way
of thinking and talking
and have resolved to lay aside
the fike-faks of company.

The town rich with domes, spires
and lofty buildings I walk much about
and sketch after the antiques;
I feast on marble ladies,

dance attendance in
the chamber of Venus, trip
a minuet with old Otho
and all those other Roman worthies.

Thus metamorphosed
learning to draw ruins to perfection
living unmolested by kirk or state
I am here like the King of Artists.

from Pandora's Light Box

The Georgian Gallery

Edinburgh has
a rage for splendid buildings
wrote Southey in 1819

columns and capitals
   William Playfair was the architect
friezes and plasterwork
   Lorimer and Inglis were the builders
balconies and ironwork
   Mr Berrie of Leith Walk made plaster models of the Capitals
three bays with coupled pilasters
   John Anderson of the Leith Foundry made the fireproof iron floor
a pair of Ionic columns
   Robert Buchan of George Street painted the interior
rich and ornate plaster decoration
   Mr Trotter of Princes Street made the display cabinets
a Greek Doric temple inside out

This is the Georgian Gallery
formerly
the Natural History Museum
built for Professor Jameson's burgeoning collection

where John Edmonstone
a freed Guyanese slave
taught Darwin taxidermy

and an early drawing
shows a tame puma
lying under a cabinet

Jameson amassed 74,000 specimens
  well-ripened seeds dried in the sun
and twice rehoused the collection
  bulbous roots
first here in 1826
  butterflies and moths with delicate and tender wings
where the structure of the rooms
  beetles of brilliant colours and lustre
remains more or less as it was –
  shells brought up by the cable in weighing anchor
a large central room
  molluscs – cuttle-fish and the inhabitants of shells
framed with an upper gallery –
  sea-water washed skeletons
and then in 1861
  every mineral from the most common clay or sand to the gem
to the new and still extant
  the sands of deserts, steppes, and rivers

museum on Chambers Street
   sands of deserts, steppes, and rivers
   of deserts, steppes, and rivers
   deserts, steppes, and rivers

This is the Georgian Gallery
formerly an exam hall
where anxious students
scratched nib over foolscap
one eye on the clock

but don't the
sprung wooden floor
and elaborate pillars
suggest a ball-room?

on the sideboard
punch-bowl spices
roast meat
sponge-cake
dancers
when a small string-band strikes up
take to the floor

the men soon smelling somewhat equine
the women of powder-masked sweat

and when the instruments fall silent
dancers leave the floor

to anxious students
students scratching nibs
nibs over foolscap
foolscap with one eye
eye on the clock
the clock more fastidious
fastidious even than the dancing-instructor
the dancing-instructor at keeping time
at keeping time two-three-four
pause two-three-four and

stop.

Summer Grasses

at Killerton we walked in silence
past dandelions already gone to seed
and summer grasses

*

at Knightshayes we walked in silence
through memories of the buzzing airman's crash
while blue dragonflies skimmed the fountain

*

at Lanhydrock we walked in silence
through formal Victorian gardens
and the newly mown graveyard

*

at Clovelly we walked in silence
through a greenwood
to a stony beach

at Overbeck's we walked in silence
high above the blue bay
on the afternoon of the longest day

*

at Castle Drogo we walked in silence
past dismantled parapets
into the orchard

*

at Stourhead we walked in silence
through 'The Shades'
and descended to the lake

*

at Croft Castle we walked in silence
from a welcome frustrated by war
to a doubly unwelcome return

at Dunham Massey we walked in silence
along the towpath to the Rope and Anchor
where the horses were commandeered

*

at the Hardmans' House we walked in silence
through the cathedral's complexities
and the bombed-out church, open to angelic skies

*

at Penrhyn Castle we walked in silence
away from cyclopean gothic
into unforgiving heat

*

at Nostell Priory we walked in silence
to the ha-ha where the music
carried, just

at Attingham Park we walked in silence
beneath the motto of the deserving rich
to Eada's only church

*

at Chirk Castle we walked in silence
past a rustic Orpheus
and a blindfold nymph

*

at Dudmaston we walked in silence
under apple-boughs
where kids were fighting over windfalls

*

at Ormesby Hall we walked in silence
from shell-shocked refugees
to prosperous suburbia

at Osterley Park we walked in silence
past Adam's transparent portico
and the Army Service Corps Mechanical Transport Depot

*

at Ightham Mote we walked in silence
on a right-of-way across private land
to a saintless church of the Commonwealth

*

at Ashridge we walked in silence
on land scarred with practice trenches
remnant deer glimpsed in the woods

*

at Whipsnade we walked in silence
between holly-hedge and mesh-fence
to a porch of oaks and a nave of limes

at Nymans we walked in silence
until it was broken by
a proprietorial thank you

*

at Bateman's we walked in silence
to a memorial naming the dead
who kept dying long after the war was over

*

at the White Cliffs of Dover we walked in silence
past holm oaks and seakale
relishing life at the edge

Cloqueliclot

We have a liking for round numbers and
Battlefields, for duty free, hand luggage,
Open borders, self drive, touchscreen smartphones.
We've come to see what's been remade, what's left.

Driving into Flanders the land flattens,
Falls into lines of poplars and pylons,
Small clusters of slow-turning wind-turbines,
Placid, calm canals the straight road bridges.

We walk in cemeteries open to
The skies or cold under oak canopies
Where body parts are interred, and the words
KNOWN UNTO GOD and UNBEKANNT recur.

What did they believe they were dying for?
Even if they were here to ask, they speak
A dead language I mouth awkwardly and
Parse with difficulty, like school Latin.

The British stones give age at time of death
(The teenagers, the men of middle age);
The German stones recall a place, *Heimat*
(Bremen, Schwerin, Neubukowitz, Husum).

Skirting fields they contested with their lives
We admire the unharvested produce –
Swollen cabbages and walls of sweetcorn,
Yellow kernels emerging from the husk.

Perhaps it's not the season but we see
No specimen of *papaver rhoeas*,
Poppy, *Mohn, coquelicot, cromlus, klaaproos,*
(the same red bloom despite these varied roots).

We hear their words in darkened rooms *I must
Tell you of what I have seen* – inspect a
Map with Poperinge's fingered absence,
Lighter touches tracing the Salient.

Here the locks were opened to inundate
The fields and halt the enemy advance;
The church we stand inside was nothing but
Rubble and two arches the moon silvered.

A track runs through the open autumn wood.
We stoop to peer inside tilting bunkers
Mossed but kept clear of ivy and bramble.
How do you pour concrete in a war zone?

I never knew (or can't remember) all
Of my grandfather's war – conscripted, gassed,
Captured, in hospital then in a camp;
His medals are silent on the matter.

A crowd has gathered at the Menin Gate
For the bugler's 'Last Post'. It ends and
During the ceremonial silence
A skein of geese honk across the twilight.

An old man plays a repetitive tune
On a horn-violin while tourist-boats
Ply the canal; you browse the market stalls,
Buy wooden shoe-lasts sized for a toddler.

High on a bell-tower I see a jackdaw
Land on a gargoyle below me. It takes
Off, drops then ascends to the spires above
Leaving me stuck here with my gravity.

Two mounds, topped with sword-cross and with needle,
Are spoil-bings from long defunct phosphate mines.
The first and last dead of Reich and Empire.
Late September sun warms a shady grove.

A horse fat with summer ambles over.
Coquelicot, says her mother, *coquelicot*.
A starling-cloud settles on a pylon.
Cloqueliclot, the girl fumbles, *cloqueliclot*.

Poperinge – Ypres – Langemark –
Bruges – St Symphorien, September 2014

Ness

The Sacred

The meadows meander,
the hillside is steep.
Now comes the spring tide,
now comes the neap.

The sweetwater salmon
loves the high seas,
the submarine dolphin
gulps in the breeze.

Columba unlocked
the fortress of Brude,
foot-weary pilgrims
crossed at the ford.

Churches arose
next to the river,
connection and barrier,
taker and giver.

The meadows meander,
the hillside is steep.
Now comes the spring tide,
now comes the neap.

Ness

Rivers hold
the oldest names

we have the word
but lack its sense

Ness might mean
now or headland

a murmuring
of running water

lake of the falls
the name of a goddess

or just a lost tongue's
word for river.

Salmon and Eel

bradan

the anadromous salmon
drifts river to ocean
follows the stars
smells its way back
to its natal river

easgann

the catadromous eel
drifts ocean to river
shifts yellow to silver
migrates (it may be)
to spawn in Sargasso

pressure holds in check the tide's pressure holds in check the headwaters'

Lochs

Chorus the dawn
at Loch nan Eun.

*

Silver glitters
Loch nan Lann.

*

The berries ripen
at Loch nan Oighreagan.

*

The snail's defences
at Loch Duntelchaig.

Grinding the grains
at Loch nam Bràthan.

*

Pass between summits
at Loch a' Bhealaich.

*

The climb is steep
from Loch ma Stac.

*

The grey breath
of Loch Liath.

Hillstreams

Allt an Fhithich,
a stream named for its ravens.

*

Allt Seileach,
a stream named for its willows.

*

Allt nan Adag,
a stream named for its stooks.

*

Allt Càrn an Doire Mhòir,
a stream named for the rocky hill where the oaks grew.

Allt Còinneag,
a stream named for its bees.

*

Allt nan Sgitheach,
a stream named for its hawthorn.

*

Allt an Dubhair,
a stream named for its shade.

*

Allt na Crìche,
a stream named for the demarcation of here and there.

Caochan Ruadh

red rill
little blind one
hidden in herbage
discovered in sound

High Pastures
Kilbride, Isle of Skye

Today the golden bough
is a trapdoor
opening into a cleft
in which the burn
sings its cold songs.

Orpheus emerges
alone and shivering,
bewildered by sunlight.
By birch and hazel,
by oak and alder,

deer, goat, eagle, curlew,
even the boar
deep in the forest dark
approach and gather
and lie before him, charmed.

The Solitary Reaper

field *raon* 野

A dissonant cry
in a large, ill-furnished house –
rather seek poetry, your portion
of land, your allies
on a mossy plain,
seek the grace of the highway.

*

melancholy *tiamhaidh* 憂

Parched with thirst
and melancholy
at the well
I melt into tears
and better feelings.

*

vale *gleann* 谷

A sparrow and blossom
of wood-sorrel in the dell
where I am fond of roaming –
fond of its sudden, hazy calm,
with sometimes puffs of soft wind.

voice *guth* 声

An act of weeping,
an act of beseeching –
and the curlew's voice
indicating
the place of an oracle.

*

spring *earrach* 春

The deer don't run,
are confident and trusting –
it's spring,
the dog-brier greens
and I am rich.

*

song *òran* 歌

A hermit
whose dress and ornaments
appear fantastic,
whose songs, orderly and becoming,
shine like gold.

hill   *cnoc*   山路

A gift of hazels
on the knoll –
and the path continues
through the whins.

Into Ettrick

the soul of one
who's found the way home
eases like water
over a stone

Marshes

The boardwalk bears us above the roots
of goat willow, crack willow, osier, sallow
buzzing with catkins.

Sentimental, anachronistic
the beech stays true to last year's shades
matched only by a last few haws.

Scots pine dance slow contortions
against pale slopes and a sky
breaking into blue.

Pitched up on the slope
the birdhide has its back
to spruce plantations.

Memorial

Here on the site of the cottage
in which James Hogg
the Ettrick Shepherd was born

stands a memorial to one
who made things up
who coined lies

none here inscribed but
a stone bench offers
a hard place to sit

to read perhaps
to contemplate a fiction
of one's choice

on either side a dog is barking
guarding the proprieties.

Potburn

An east wind in spring time
brings snow to the fell,
so far down the valley
is too far to dwell.

The old house is solid,
outbuildings crumble,
abstracted lichen
patterns the harling.

Rain on the roof
drummed through his dreams.
The trees are about to
rip open their seams.

Over Phawhope

Just below Ettrick Head
across the Entertrona Burn
the blessed sun was in heaven
although obscured by clouds.

A simple shelter maintained,
two stone buildings and a sentinel pine;
a lonely and dismal situation,
a last retreat of the spirits of the glen.

Will O'Phaup's unsought encounters,
Gilmartin's shadowy comings and goings,
Davie Balfour set for Cramond,
Boston's search for still waters.

Church

Veined with shadow-branches
the tower of 1824,
a 1619 MEMENTO MORI
in the outer wall.

firm as a stone
unstable as water
memory, a leaking vessel

Leading to the laird's loft
a double outside staircase;
inside are ordered pews,
pulpit and harmonium.

as the water of a river
is still coming
however much has passed

Boston's trig memorial,
the grass is starred with celandine,
Hogg's harp kept clear of moss,
primrose flowers by the dyke.

grant me a harp
NATURAE DONUM
I ask no more

The Ash Grove

a *springtime* ash, whose leaves emerge from black
an *unlocked* ash, so profligate with keys
a *mourning* ash, its branches heaped on pyres
a *lettered* ash, in the alphabet of trees
a *hedgerow* ash, which twists among the briars
a *spreading* ash, in summer's heat a bield
a *sporting* ash, to take the shinty field

a *warlike* ash, for arrows and for spears
a *lightning* ash, and flame that flash provides
a *hanging* ash, a shade of dule and tears
a *timeless* ash, the horse which Odin rides
a *steam-bent* ash, which hoops the barrel staves
a *buoyant* ash, a charm against the waves
a *blighted* ash, whose crown is dying back

Willow Labyrinth, Falkland

now your steps to here have led
sit within the woven shade

just outside this pliant wall
crowstep clocktower steeple hill

in the future bear in mind
the twists of labyrinthine time

What is a tree?

What is a lime?

A steady buzz
of honey bees
settles summer.

*

What is a sycamore?

Coming late to the party
its grain flames into song.

*

What is a birch?

Wields a new broom
but keeps things light –
sociable with its own
and a welcoming host.

What is a rowan?

Berries threaded
(the birds have plenty) –
an amulet against winter.

*

What is a beech?

An expanding archive
of autographs
and declarations.

*

What is a horse-chestnut?

Between sticky buds
and spiky husks, candles
bob like boats at sea.

What is a yew?

A golden shimmer.
A pillared shade.
A natural temple.
A resurrection.

*

What is an ash?

Black buds release
a purple haze, late
leaves shadow silver.

*

What is a spruce?

A quick grower
reaching for the sky –
once felled, it flies.

What is an elder?

Better for bellows and pipes
than fuel, it's a stinker –
though cordial too.

*

What is a cherry?

Fateful encounters –
pale blossom, dark fruit,
heartwood, sweet smoke.

*

What is a Scots pine?

The sound of a fiddle
(the resin, the rosin)
bowed on a watertight boat.

Anything But
National Fruit Collection, Brogdale, Kent

chilly April –
an Early Bird
at the Sun Inn

chilly April –
Pyrus Chanticleer
has yet to crow

chilly April –
the Blue Prolific
is anything but

chilly April –
Zwemmers Fruehzwetsche
and one bee

chilly April –
Prunus Stella
unconstellated

chilly April –
one magpie
in a fallow field

Crailing Pomona

Ard Cairn Russet

With keeping
an Irish banana
turns cloyingly sweet.

*

Arthur Turner

An agreeable prolific
of uncertain origin –
watch him at blossom-time.

*

Beurré Hardy

In the Luxembourg gardens
the shade is scented
with rose-water.

Black Mickey

From one surviving seedling
a Scot propagated
the McIntosh apple.

*

Catherine

A sweet Combs cooker
found in the grounds...
live and let live.

*

Catillac

In some mouths autocratic,
monstrous – in others
a goddess's breasts.

Concorde

A marriage announced
in a mid-Atlantic accent,
vanilla-sweet.

*

Discovery

As one-armed Mr Dummer's wife
broke her ankle, this seedling sat
in sack, with frost forecast – but...

*

Early Julyan

Authorities agree
this Scot is brisk –
carpe diem.

Egremont Russet

Crushed fern scent,
smoky after keeping –
late autumn's richest.

*

Gloucester Morceau

Far from the Cotswolds
a titbit translated
becomes a glutton.

*

Hessle

A freckled northerner
hardy enough for almost
every situation and part.

Irish Peach

From Sligo shellsoil
difficult to capture at its
best straight from the tree.

*

James Grieve

Raised on Leith Walk
by Dickson's nurserymen,
father to Greensleeves and Katy.

*

Louise Bonne Of Jersey

From Normandy in fact
before the Revolution –
upright and reliable.

Peasgood Nonsuch

Raised from a pip
sown in a pot
by the future Mrs P.

*

Pitmaston Pineapple

Intensely flavoured
in good years
musk and honey.

*

Red Devil

The devil
disliking deer
decamped.

White Melrose

Remembering the riverside
orchards raised and tended
by white-robed monks.

*

Yellow Ingestrie

Its beautiful habit of drooping...
decorative, ideal
for a kissing bough.

*

Removing the crown,
so others might thrive

    pruning

Castle Garden of Water to Beyond

january
LATENCY

february
LENGTHENING

march
GRAVITY

april
FILIGREE

may
REMEMBERED

june
REVEALED (CONCEALED)

july
WITHOUT RESTRAINT

august
TEARS

september
LIMINAL

october
BLUSTER

november
WHATEVER

december
REVERIE

While yet we may

五月雨

samidare
      May rains –
ay, think on that, my heart, and cease to stir

卯の花

unohana
      small white flowers –
for thou art with me here

薄

susuki
      sedge –
a presence that disturbs me

夢

yume
      dream –
these gleams of past existence

短冊

tanzaku
      a poem –
surpassing grace to me hath been vouchsafed

はやぶさ

hayabusa
      sweeping falcon –
trackless hills by mists bewildered

滝

taki
    waterfall –
high the transport, great the joy

秋風

akikaze
    autumn wind –
in that sequestered valley

細道

hosomichi
    back road –
affecting thoughts and dear remembrances

松

matsu

    the pine –
rooted now so deeply in my mind

ほととぎす

hototogisu

    cuckoo –
how fast that length of way was left behind

閑かさ

shizukasa

    stillness –
nor should this, perchance, pass unrecorded

酒

sake

    rice-wine –
blessings spread around me like a sea

夏山

natsuyama

    summer mountain –
made for itself and happy in itself

隻鳬

sekifu

    a single wild duck –
in calm thought reflected

雪

yuki

    snow –
a time of rapture!

月

tsuki

    moon –
sweetly 'mid the gloom

松

matsu

    the pine –
abundant cause to speak thanks

短冊

tanzaku
　　a poem –
a pittance from strict time

細道

hosomichi
　　back road –
a depth of vale below, a height of hills above

五月雨

samidare
　　May rains –
craft of delicate Spirits

ほととぎす

hototogisu

    cuckoo –

for such loss abundant recompense

薄

susuki

    sedge –

somewhat of a sad perplexity

雪

yuki

    snow –

the weary weight of all this unintelligible world

はやぶさ

hayabusa

    sweeping falcon –

by his fire the Hermit sits alone

秋風

akikaze

    autumn wind –

within the Vale of Nightshade

酒

sake

    rice-wine –

content with my own modest pleasures

隻鳧

sekifu

    a single wild duck –
I must tread on shadowy ground

閑かさ

shizukasa

    stillness –
to the brim my heart was full

夏山

natsuyama

    summer mountain –
breath and everlasting motion

夢

yume

    dream –
clouds that sail on winds

月

tsuki

    moon –
all the sweetness of a common dawn

卯の花

unohana

    small white flowers –
we sank each into commerce with his private thoughts

滝

taki

    waterfall –

in the blessed hours of early love

薄

susuki

    sedge –

it was in truth an ordinary sight

月

tsuki

    moon –

the dignities of plain occurrence

隻鳧

sekifu

    a single wild duck –
with eager pace, and no less eager thoughts

短冊

tanzaku

    a poem –
and these my exhortations!

五月雨

samidare

    May rains –
unfading recollections

酒

sake

    rice-wine –
drenched in empyrean light

はやぶさ

hayabusa

    sweeping falcon –
a centre, come from wheresoe'er you will

卯の花

unohana

    small white flowers –
what strange utterance

細道

hosomichi
　　　back road –
the orange sky of evening died away

夢

yume
　　　dream –
felt in the blood, and felt along the heart

滝

taki
　　　waterfall –
these wild ecstacies

ほととぎす
hototogisu
    cuckoo –
an index of delight

夏山
natsuyama
    summer mountain –
at my feet the ground appeared to brighten

松
matsu
    the pine –
a breath of fragrance

雪

yuki

    snow –

stern was the face of nature

閑かさ

shizukasa

    stillness –

a blended holiness of earth and sky

秋風

akikaze

    autumn wind –

our future course all plain to sight

Come to the garden which might seem dead and view
the empty house, the dripping ferns and mosses;
between the clouds an unexpected blue
unshades the hollows and the paths' criss-crosses.

Accept those dabs of yellow, the lichen-greys
that nuzzle birch and hazel like a breeze.
The last rosehips still haven't lost their red.
They cluster like a garland round your head.

Don't miss the bank where chanterelles are rife
or the tiny plums, dark and sour and solemn
and gently spool into the face of autumn
whatever still remains of this green life.

after Stefan Georg

A Christmas List

a muddy path
and a hot bath

an *ushanka*, thank you
and a hand of canasta

weight-bearing ice
and a throw of the dice

a tale of Troy
and a principal boy

a pulled cork
and a tuning-fork

a thrush in the trees
and antifreeze

Midwinter Wishes

I wish you midwinter darkness
the better to see the stars.

I wish you midwinter silence
the better to hear yourself think.

I wish you a midwinter forest
to lose your way in.

I wish you a midwinter fog
to attend to what's closest.

I wish you midwinter snow
as a page for your footprints.

I wish you midwinter ice
so the thaw when it comes
cracks all the louder.

Afterword

I'VE WORKED FREELANCE as a poet for over a decade now. That doesn't mean I spend my time writing poems – in fact to make a living I'm kept busy running workshops in schools and community settings. But from time to time I've received commissions, or made my own writing opportunities, and this book gathers together the resulting poems, almost all written with a public outcome in mind. Many involved collaboration; having started my working life in theatre, that most collaborative of disciplines, I find poems emerge from conversation and shared endeavour as much as from meditative silence.

The other main bodies of writing I undertook during this time were two journey projects with Alec Finlay: *The Road North*, when we let ourselves be guided through Scotland by the 17th century Japanese poet Basho, and *Out of Books*, a version of Boswell and Johnson's *Tour of the Hebrides* in 1773. Those experiences – which connected walking and reading, focused on locality, and viewed Scotland through the usefully distorting prism of other literatures and languages – inform much of the work here.

These poems have been published in various ways – in books and on blogs, as cards and prints, on benches and botanical labels, as sound recordings and projected images. The longer sequences are presented more or less in chronological order; some of these I've revised, cutting poems that felt superfluous, and at times rewriting for the page. The following paragraphs will, I hope, offer some context.

'An Alphabet of Blues' was written for ~in the fields (Stefan Baumberger and Nicole Heidtke). We were introduced by a mutual friend, Alice Bain, who noticed a connection between my 'flyleaf' poems, written actually or notionally in books, and their sculptural work 'ink', five clear glass globes each partly filled with blue ink, which re-present to the viewer handwritten inscriptions from printed books. Undertaking the given task – responding to the artists and their artwork, their blue – I used a given form, the alphabet, and found the combined constraints evoked memories in a way that more direct approaches often fail to do.

Combinations were the key to another work by ~in the fields, *Yen to See Distant Places*. They had adapted 19th century engravings (mainly from Scott's *Provincial Antiquities and Picturesque Scenery of Scotland*) to create three sets of new images – fifteen 'sublime' backgrounds, fifteen 'beautiful' middlegrounds and fifteen 'picturesque' foregrounds – so any background can be combined with any middleground and any foreground to create a composite image (there are 3,375 possible combinations). To accompany each new image I composed a short poetic line (often drawing on Scott's poems), which similarly can be combined to create a composite verse. I thought of the verses as a kind of schematic haiku, so the work, with its generational possibilities and its particular sensibility, became a 'Romantic haiku machine'.

'While yet we may' is another kind of 'haiku machine'. It was written for *Walking Poets*, an exhibition linking Wordsworth and Basho. Their differences – of language, landscape, religion, poetic forms – are more striking than their similarities. To connect them I borrowed the simple combinatory method of a 'variable construction' by the late Gael Turnbull, consisting of two sets of cards, one of 28 nouns, the other of 112 qualifying phrases; any phrase could be combined with any noun, and these combinations made up the poem, shuffled new each time he read it. My measures were seventeen and fifty-one; seventeen words from Basho, matching the syllables in a haiku, and three times that to give a range of Wordsworthian qualifiers.

'Pandora's Light Box' was also written for a gallery setting. Artlink Edinburgh and Lothians offer gallery tours for people with a visual impairment, which rely on careful verbal descriptions of the gallery space and artworks. Could such descriptions be extended, or transformed, into artworks in their own right? When I explored the Talbot Rice Gallery at the University of Edinburgh with a group of participants with a visual impairment, I was struck by their emphasis on sound and smell. One said, 'smells evoke memories you didn't know you had', and the parquet floor prompted their recall of the mingled smells of floor polish, perfume and sweat at regimental dances.

When I was asked to write about contemporary Edinburgh and imperial Rome for a World Heritage Day event, I cast around for a link. The Romans didn't impose themselves in Scotland, the Antonine Wall proving less durable than Hadrian's further south, and I recall little of my school Latin. The obvious link was the seven hills each city is built on. Walking Edinburgh's, I considered Romans and barbarians, and the walls that separate them. The number seven suggested a poetic measure, while the question-and-answer form gave me scope to explore classical and contemporary themes by way of simple lists.

The months of the year offer another measure; twelve suggests completeness, like the alphabet's A to Z, but moving circularly rather than in a straight line. In early 2014 I decided to visit the Japanese garden at Lauriston Castle in Edinburgh once a month. The garden sits on the shores of the Firth of Forth, and its Japanese name translates literally as 'Castle Garden of Water to Beyond'. The verses again use a simple combinatory method. Like Ian Hamilton Finlay's 'one-word poems', they consist of a title (the name of the month) and a qualifier; they weren't conceived as a sequence, but I found myself writing one or more during each visit, and made this selection at the end of the year.

Silence has to find its own measure. 'Summer Grasses' was written for *there were our own there were the others*, devised by Alec Finlay for summer 2014 to mark the centenary of the outbreak of the First World War. At twenty-three National

Trust properties, all of which had a connection to the war (a house used as a hospital, grounds used as a training camp, a son who enlisted and was killed), I led a silent memorial walk, bookended by a pair of poems from the past century on the theme of conflict. These walks were unexpectedly moving; after one, a volunteer, due to thank everyone for coming, found himself choked with tears and unable to speak. In September I visited First World War graveyards, battlefields and memorials in Belgium. The landscape was striking in its ordinariness; undulating farmland crisscrossed by roads and railways, punctuated by pylons and telegraph poles. I remember my grandfather telling me about his wartime experiences when I was a child, but they felt out of reach, as distant as Basho's Japan or Roman legions by the Forth, a distance 'Cloqueliclot' attempts to fathom.

A day similarly shadowed – or illuminated – by the past was the one I spent in the Ettrick Valley with the painter Andrew Mackenzie (Easter Monday, as it happened). I knew Ettrick from books: those of James Hogg, 'The Ettrick Shepherd', and Stevenson's *Kidnapped*, which opens with David Balfour leaving the inland valley to seek his inheritance. Andrew knew the area, acted as guide and set our itinerary, which the sequence of poems matches. He later produced four silverpoint drawings, reworked as etchings, two of which relate to 'Marshes'; the others show the house at Potburn, and the churchyard's 'shadow-branches'. Our collaboration was the shared experience of the trip; we composed separately, but the common content of our respective works lets them sit well together.

The 'Ness' poems were written for the sculptor Mary Bourne, who had been commissioned to make work for the Inverness riverside. They refer to the River Ness and its vast catchment area, a network of rivers, lochs and streams reaching inland from Loch Ness. These have Gaelic names, whose meaning is opaque to most English speakers, myself included. During *The Road North*, Alec Finlay and I had started looking into the meaning of Scottish place-names; he'd since researched and written on the subject in books like *Some Colour Trends* (2014). Understanding such place-names clarifies our view of landscape, prompting us to seek out colours, trees, creatures, culture, history.

I found Malcolm Maclennan's Gaelic–English dictionary (1925) a useful source-book, as he often gives Gaelic words extended and evocative English glosses. I returned to Maclennan for 'The Solitary Reaper', written for a second exhibition linking Wordsworth and Basho. Its title comes from a Wordsworth poem in which he describes hearing with delight a 'solitary Highland Lass' singing in a language he cannot understand – Gaelic. I chose seven words from Wordsworth's text, and their equivalents in Gaelic and Japanese (the latter can also be found in one or more poems by Basho). Starting with Maclennan's English definitions of the seven Gaelic words, together with those of a few other words on the same page, I stitched the poems together. (By way of example, 'hill *cnoc* 山路' draws on the following words and definitions: *cnò*, a nut, a filbert; *cnoc*, a knoll, an eminence; *cnoid*, a splendid present; *conair*, a path, way; *conas*, furze, whins; strife, wrangling.) I fancy the poems as translations of the reaper's song, made by a poet familiar with Basho's work.

Ken Cockburn
March 2018

Notes

'Bob the Roman' is adapted from letters written by the architect Robert Adam (1728–1792) from Rome between 1755 and 1757.

'Crailing Pomona': my main sources were *The New Book of Apples* (ed. Richards and Morgan,1993), *A Handbook of Hardy Fruits: Apples and Pears*, EA Bunyard, 1920) and *Herefordshire Pomona* (Hogg and Bull, 1876–85).

'Credit': the episode is from Book 7 of *The Odyssey*.

'Into Ettrick': the artist William Johnstone (1897–1981) lived at Potburn after he retired from teaching in London. Over Phawhope, near the head of valley, is associated with James Hogg's grandfather, Will O'Phaup (1691–1775). At Ettrick Church there is a well-tended memorial to Thomas Boston (1676–1732), a Presbyterian minister and theologian. The epigraph ('the soul of one...') is adapted from a sentence in Josephine Hart's novel *Damage* (1991), quoted in the exhibition catalogue *William Johnstone: Marchlands* (2012). The late Karl Miller, referring to Hogg's cousin, James Laidlaw, wrote, 'poor Hogg made things up and got more money for his lies, according to Laidlaw, than Thomas Boston ever did for his sermons'.

'Over Phawhope' borrows from passages in Hogg's *The Shepherd's Calendar* (1837). The first two italicised sections of 'Church' are adapted from Boston's *Human Nature in its Fourfold State* (1720); the third borrows from Hogg's *The Queen's Wake* (1813). *Naturae Donum*, a gift of nature, was Hogg's motto.

A recording of 'Pandora's Light Box' read by myself and Lorna Irvine is available at soundcloud.com (search for 'Pandora's Light Box'). For those interested in the building of the Georgian Gallery, see Andrew Fraser's *The Building of Old College* (EUP, 1989).

'What is a tree?': 'Yew' borrows from Wordsworth's 'Yew Trees'.

Some other books published by **LUATH PRESS**

On the Flyleaf
Ken Cockburn
ISBN 9781906307189 PBK £8.99

On the Flyleaf dwells on the connection between people, places, languages and literature. Inspired by inscriptions, graffiti and scribbled notes on the flyleaves of books – Ovid, a guide book, a superhero comic – these poems interweave travel, home and love, while quietly subverting notions of standing and rank in literature. Handling both the narrative poem and the haiku with equal skill, Cockburn observes and probes the ways in which we interpret the world with an uncluttered eye.

It is refreshing to read contemporary poetry of such rare grace and compassion... a welcome contribution to the literature of our nomadic century.
TOM HUBBARD, FIFE LINES

One of the principal strengths of Cockburn's poetry is its exploration of the life that is contained in seemingly trivial, small or uneventful moments. The result is gentle, meditative poetry that is occasionally opaque but often subtly powerful.
ALAN RAWES, SCOTTISH LITERARY JOURNAL

Letters to My Mother and other mothers

Bashabi Fraser
ISBN 9781910745144 PBK £8.99

They forego promotion and pay packets.
They stay at home. They are night watchers
Who feed and rock and calm to sleep
They tie their precious gifts to their back
Or stagger in tired pride, pushing our future
They are the bravest soldiers – marching on.
– Mothers All

How does our relationship with our mothers shape the people we become? Does the experience of motherhood change us? Bashabi Fraser commemorates her mother and the conversations they would have together. Exploring themes of motherhood, empowerment, love and loss, the acclaimed poet draws on her Indian and British life experience, engaging with hard-hitting current issues such as climate change, war and the prevalence of violence against women worldwide.

A son questions his mother's love after she has learned about his violent deeds. The biblical Eve is shown as a liberator. A daughter of India demands justice from her society. Fraser's powerful, passionate poetry contemplates the experience of motherhood and celebrates the life of her own mother and of other mothers.

An Leabhar Liath/The Light Blue Book: 500 Years of Gaelic love and transgressive verse

Ed. Peter MacKay and Iain MacPherson
ISBN 9781910745472 HBK £20

The 2017 Saltire Research Book of the Year and winner of of the 2016 Donald Meek Award.

This collection, covering 500 years of transgressive Gaelic poetry with new English translations, breaks the mould for anthologies of Gaelic verse. It offers poems that are erotic, rude, seditious and transgressive; that deal with love, sex, the body, politics and violent passion; and that are by turns humorous, disturbing, shocking and enlightening. In scholarly introductions in Gaelic and English the editors give contexts for the creation, transmission and value of these poems, as historical documents, as joyous – or tragic – works of art, as products of a culture and counter-cultures that have survived centuries of neglect, suppression or threats of being 'burned by the hand of the common executioner'. After reading this book, you won't think of Gaelic culture in quite the same way ever again.

North End of Eden
Christine De Luca
ISBN 9781906817329 PBK £8.99

A polar projection changes foo we figure oot wir world. Shetland isna banished tae a box i da Moray Firt or left oot aa tagidder – ta scale up da rest – but centre stage.

Christine De Luca's poetry creates a sense of the beauty and spareness of Shetland, the contradictory space and smallness of the island; and a feeling for people. These poems explore concepts of identity, home and belonging, and of our connection with the land. Drawing inspiration from medicine, history and religious and pagan legends, from modern and ancient sources, De Luca awakens reader to the beauty of the language and the landscape of the most northern part of Britain; yet there is no sense of isolation. She explores the folktales and values home-grown in Shetland in terms of the wider world, from Russia to Canada.

In this collection Christine de Luca shows herself to be not only a heavyweight poet in her own right but also a trailblazer for the rest of us.
ELIZABETH RIMMER, NORTHWORDS NOW

The Winter Book
Alan Riach
ISBN 9781910745939 PBK £8.99

The Winter Book begins on the ice and ends at the well at the world's end.

Dark castles of bad management and wasted resources are opposed by the forces of art, the virtues of openness, a gathering sense that borders are sometimes precious things that need to be protected, and that travelling across and beyond them is equally vital.

…full of big poems which encompass a range of experience, engaging with ideas, situations, places, and the why of it. Political anger is poured into strong, argumentative, emotionally engaging poems: no easy task.
GERRIE FELLOWS

The poems in The Winter Book *connect people, places and culture across geographies, nationally in Scotland and internationally in global, political contexts of loss and affi rmation, sorrow and anger, personal and public worlds, as memories fl ow into history.*
DOUGLAS GIFFORD

Fishing for Ghosts

Mike Harding

ISBN 9781910745854 PBK £9.99

In this new collection, Harding casts his poetic line to retrieve ghosts from the near and more distant past, his eyes and ears caught by fragments snagged in his visual and aural memory. A lifetime of listening, observing, thinking and reflecting produces poems that tell stories in his own voice; at times amused, bemused, angry or simply taken by the transient beauty of light in nature or a splash of colour in an urban environment.

Harding is a natural storyteller and, like all true storytellers, his direct language engages listener and reader alike in the recognition that their own poems may also be waiting to be retrieved from the seemingly random.

Some poems make you smile, others make you think, and all of them make you take notice.
AMAZON REVIEW

Mike looks behind the walls, gets into the words and music. These poems were written at the hearth, were written from the heart. They stay with me.
CHRISTY MOORE (on *Connemara Cantos*)

Washing Hugh MacDiarmid's Socks

Magi Gibson

ISBN 9781910745472 HBK £20

Magi Gibson, a prize-winning poet, explores what it is to be a fully engaged human in today's confusing world. These poems are insightful, joyful, witty, tender and yes, at times, rude. Two women in a punch-up in Glasgow's West End. A man stepping off a tenement roof on a snowy morning. An angry neighbour. A letter of solidarity to Sappho. Not to mention those dirty socks. Or that poem with the intriguing title, 'V****A'.

Tender and compassionate... Catches all the qualities of Gibson's best writing. Metaphorically juxtaposing the skeletons in her cupboard with the ghosts in her attic Gibson is a joy to read.
THE NATIONAL

Details of these and other books published by Luath Press can be found at:

www.luath.co.uk

Luath Press Limited

committed to publishing well written books worth reading

LUATH PRESS takes its name from Robert Burns, whose little collie Luath (*Gael.*, swift or nimble) tripped up Jean Armour at a wedding and gave him the chance to speak to the woman who was to be his wife and the abiding love of his life. Burns called one of the 'Twa Dogs' Luath after Cuchullin's hunting dog in Ossian's *Fingal*. Luath Press was established in 1981 in the heart of Burns country, and is now based a few steps up the road from Burns' first lodgings on Edinburgh's Royal Mile. Luath offers you distinctive writing with a hint of unexpected pleasures.

Most bookshops in the UK, the US, Canada, Australia, New Zealand and parts of Europe, either carry our books in stock or can order them for you. To order direct from us, please send a £sterling cheque, postal order, international money order or your credit card details (number, address of cardholder and expiry date) to us at the address below. Please add post and packing as follows: UK – £1.00 per delivery address; overseas surface mail – £2.50 per delivery address; overseas airmail – £3.50 for the first book to each delivery address, plus £1.00 for each additional book by airmail to the same address. If your order is a gift, we will happily enclose your card or message at no extra charge.

Luath Press Limited
543/2 Castlehill
The Royal Mile
Edinburgh EH1 2ND
Scotland
Telephone: +44 (0)131 225 4326 (24 hours)
Email: sales@luath. co.uk
Website: www. luath.co.uk